The Prayer Shawl
Wrapped in God's Love

Greater
Purpose
Press

Written by Susan Fitzsimonds • Illustrated by Mary Gregg Byrne

MW01153408

This is a work of fiction. Names, characters, places, and incidents either are products of the author's imagination or are used fictitiously. Any resemblance to actual events, locales, or persons, living or dead, is entirely coincidental.

The Prayer Shawl: Wrapped in God's Love

Copyright © 2014 by Susan Fitzsimonds

Layout and cover design by Jacqueline L. Challiss Hill
Illustrations by Mary Gregg Byrne   Illustrations created with water colors

Printed in Canada

All rights reserved. No part of this publication may be reproduced or transmitted in any form by any means, electronic or mechanical, including photocopy, recording, or any other information storage and retrieval system, without permission in writing from the publisher.

Scripture taken from the Holy Bible, New International Version ®, NIV ®. Copyright © 1973, 1978, 1984 by International Bible Society.

Summary: A young girl discovers the power and love of receiving and giving prayer shawls.
Library of Congress Cataloging-in-Publication Data
Fitzsimonds, Susan
The Prayer Shawl: Wrapped in God's Love/Susan Fitzsimonds–First Edition
ISBN-13: 978-1-938326-19-6
1. Prayer shawls. 2. Christianity.
I. Fitzsimonds, Susan II. Title
Library of Congress Control Number: 2014930282

Greater Purpose Press is an imprint of Nelson Publishing & Marketing
366 Welch Road, Northville, MI 48167
www.nelsonpublishingandmarketing.com
(248) 735-0418

This book is dedicated to the prayer shawl ministry at Faith Covenant Church and the women who give their time and talents to this service. Your commitment to praying for others and sharing this symbol of God's love is a blessing to many.

To Peyton, Keira, and Leah. May you always feel surrounded by His love no matter what life brings.

I'd like to thank Nelson Publishing & Marketing for their dedication to this project. Thanks to Marian Nelson and Kris Yankee for their hard work, support, and encouragement.

Thanks to Mary Gregg Byrne for illustrating so beautifully a project that is so dear to my heart.

I'd like to thank my parents for raising me in a home that was built on the solid foundation of God's word. In addition, their constant love and support have helped me accomplish what I never thought possible.

I'd also like to acknowledge my appreciation for my husband. I am so lucky to have him in my life. Thanks for all the fun and laughter you bring to my life.

Most of all, the One who deserves my utmost appreciation is Jesus Christ. The more I learn, the more wonderful He becomes. I am thankful that the God of Heaven has woven every stitch of my life more perfectly than I could ever imagine.

Photo by Douglas Berg

Dear Reader,
My church began our prayer shawl ministry in 2005 and has been blessing individuals with this beautiful symbol of God's love ever since. Our ministry was started by an incredible woman named Betsy Rocket. Betsy was led to begin this ministry after hearing about it from the prayer shawl originators, Janet Severi Bristow and Victoria Galo, who began their ministry in 1998.

"Shawls...made for centuries, universal and embracing,
symbolic of an inclusive, unconditionally loving God.
They wrap, enfold, comfort, cover, give solace,
mother, hug, shelter, beautify.
Those who have received these shawls have been uplifted and affirmed,
as if given wings to fly above their troubles..."
Janet Severi Bristow 1998

I was personally touched by the impact of this ministry in 2010. A very close friend of mine had her world turned upside down when her husband (then 38) was diagnosed with inoperable brain cancer. As a friend, I wanted to help but did not know what to do. Sure cooking meals or helping with daily tasks are great, but I wanted to do more. I quickly realized only the hand of God can carry someone through such heart-wrenching moments. I had a shawl made for her, and I told her that when she felt alone, weak, scared, or even mad to always remember God's love can conquer all. The best gift I could give her in the darkest moments of her life was to pray for her, her husband, and their three small children. A prayer shawl is a symbol of God's unfailing love and it is made prayerfully for each recipient so that they may feel His presence in the midst of any difficulty.

For more information about the original prayer shawl ministry, visit www.shawlministry.com.

My grandmother loves knitting.
She made a shawl for me.
She told me it was made with love,
as special as can be.

She said, "It's not just any shawl; it's made to show God's love,
the kind that fills your soul and only comes from up above."

*"God has poured out his love
into our hearts by the
Holy Spirit, whom he has given us."*
Romans 5:5

"How can that be?" I said to her. "It's just a bunch of string!"
But at that time I didn't know the joy that it would bring.

"You see," said Grandma, "while I knit, I pray with all my heart.
This gift will show you God is there and ready to impart."

"...neither height nor depth, nor anything else in all
creation, will be able to separate us from the love of
God that is in Jesus Christ our Lord." Romans 8:39

She told me that throughout my life, when I'm feeling down,
to wrap up in this special shawl and feel God's love abound.

Then she said, "If you can't pray,
don't worry what to do.
Just remember I'll be here; I'm doing it for you."

"I urge, then, first of all, that requests, prayers,
intercession, and thanksgiving be made for everyone."
1Timothy 2:1

Many times I used my shawl when I felt joy or pain.
I slowly learned that through it all His love remains the same.
His plan is always so much more than we can ever see,
so put your trust in Jesus and let Him bring you peace.

"Trust in him at all times, O people; pour out your hearts to him, for God is our refuge." Psalm 62:8

It wasn't long 'til I felt down. Some kids were mean at school.
Teasing me about my faults was making them feel cool.

I felt so crushed. I felt alone. I couldn't wait to go.
I found my shawl and curled up tight as soon as I got home.

Then suddenly I felt assured; I would not be alone.
For there is One who walks with me when others cast a stone.
This gave me courage and the will to stand up straight and tall,
to face each challenge as it came, no matter big or small.

"The Lord is with me;
I will not be afraid.
What can man do to me?"
Psalm 118:6

Another time I tried my best but didn't make the team.
Not feeling like I measure up had hurt my self-esteem.
So I began to wonder if I'd ever feel secure
in who I was or what I did, was feeling so unsure.

That night when I got home I was fighting back the tears.
I went upstairs and shut my door and told God all my fears.
I grabbed my shawl and wrapped up tight, but didn't say a thing.
I closed my eyes and listened for the voice of reasoning.

"The Lord is my strength and my shield;
my heart trusts in him, and I am helped."
Psalm 28:7

I know when God is speaking 'cause I feel His awesome peace.
My worry, doubt, and hopelessness begin to slowly cease.

He didn't promise perfect lives to those who follow Him;
He promised that He'd shine His light when all things looked so dim.

"And the Peace of God,
which transcends all understanding,
will guard your hearts
and your minds in Christ Jesus."
Philippians 4:7

Years went by, my life was fine,
but that all quickly changed.
A broken heart has crushed my hopes,
my plans now rearranged.

My prayer time's getting longer now.
My shawl stays on my lap.
I beg the Lord to mend my heart
and simply bring him back.

No answer comes my way this time.
"Where are you, God?" I pray.
"This hurt is way too much to bear;
please take it all away."

Then one night, deep in prayer,
I heard Him say, "Trust me!
You can't see now, but I have plans
to bring you love and peace."

"'For I know the plans I have for you,' declares the Lord,
'plans to prosper you and not to harm you, plans to
give you hope and a future.'" Jeremiah 29:11

As time went on my life was full of loss and praise and hope.
I wonder if my grandma knew how much she helped me cope.
The best part was that through it all, she taught me I should pray,
even if I did not think I had a lot to say.

"Be joyful always; pray continually; give thanks in all circumstances, for this is God's will for you in Jesus Christ."
1 Thessalonians 5:16-18

"Grandma, can you teach me how to knit with that much care?"
"It's not about the knitting. It is all about the prayer.
Each shawl I make is personal. I'm praying while I knit.
This gift is made to show you that His love's a perfect fit."

I started making prayer shawls so I could share His word.
I wanted to give out this gift and make sure others heard.
There is such comfort when we know that God is always near.
He covers us in His great hope and takes away our fears.

"In the same way, let your light shine before men,
that they may see your good deeds and praise your Father in heaven."
Matthew 5:16

My friend was sick, and so I thought she needs to feel His power
and needs His love to guide her as she meets each passing hour.
I made a shawl and told her when she felt too weak to pray,
wrap yourself inside His arms and you will feel His strength.

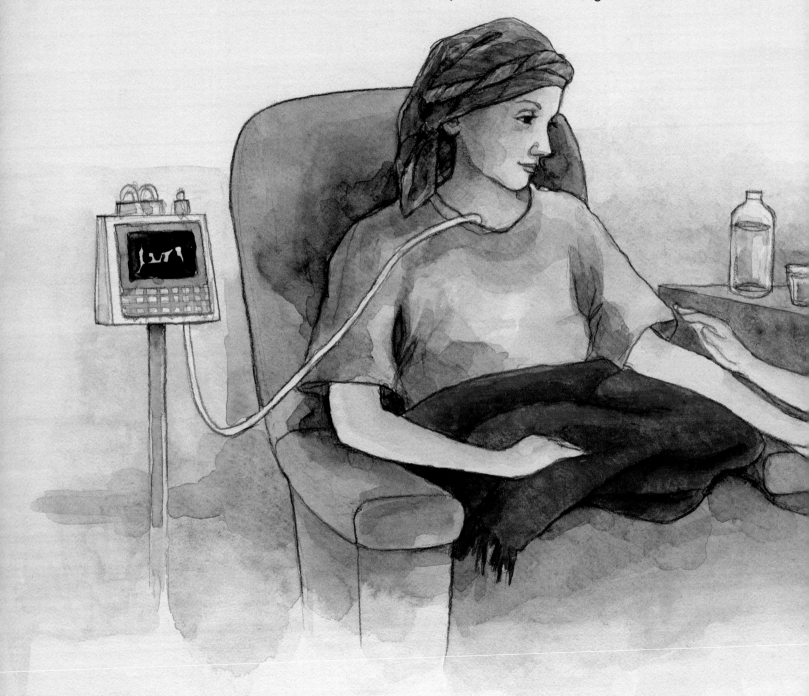

I'm sure it's made a difference. It's comforting to know
when you don't have the words to pray that others will do so.
Her shawl is precious to her; it symbolizes faith.
It reminds her that God's loving hand is there to keep her safe.

"Now faith is being sure
of what we hope for
and certain
of what we do not see."
Hebrews 11:1

My neighbor lost his job and I made a shawl for him.

Even though he still felt down it made him smile again.

Then I learned about a friend whose life was full of fears.

Her shawl was meant to give her strength and take away her tears.

I knew a girl who broke a bone.
Her leg was in a cast.
I knitted and I asked the Lord
to heal her very fast.

"But I will restore you to health and heal your wounds." Jeremiah 30:17

I was having so much fun while blessing all their lives.
But when I got that awful call, I ran right to her side.

My grandma isn't feeling well and I don't have a shawl.
How can this be? I need to help. I started to just bawl.

I got some yarn. I sat with her. I knitted and I prayed.
Lord, thank you for my grandma. I'm glad I know she's saved.

"For it is by grace you have been saved,
through faith—and this is not from yourselves,
it is the gift of God." Ephesians 2:8

When it was done,
I covered us in God's amazing love.
He took her home to be with
Him in heaven up above.

"For the Lord is good and his love
endures forever; his faithfulness
continues through all generations."
Psalm 100:5

I'll bet you there is someone else who needs my grandma's shawl.
Please pass it on so that God's love is felt by one and all.

Susan Fitzsimonds began her career as an educator thirteen years ago as a second grade teacher. During this time, she pursued her master's in counseling from Oakland University. She obtained a K–12 counseling endorsement, a counseling license, and specialization in child and adolescent therapy. She worked for eight years as an elementary counselor. Susan has a passion for helping children increase their self-esteem, overcome adversity, and learn skills for dealing with difficult situations. Susan's first book, *The Hero in Me*, teaches children about dealing with bullying. This book received four national awards including a Mom's Choice® and Teacher's Choice℠ award. Susan presents to children of all ages about how to be a hero in tough situations. For more information about Susan, please visit her website, www.suefitzbooks.com.

Mary Gregg Byrne lives in Bellingham, Washington. She reads, writes, and creates art. Mary teaches watercolor classes and illustrates children's books. She watches her garden and the children grow. She walks in the mountains. She cherishes her friends. Mary enjoys the changing light of the seasons and of her life. For more information about Mary and her art, please visit www.marygreggbyrne.com.